CHRISTIAN HEROES: THEN & NOW

CAMERON TOWNSEND

Unit Study

Curriculum Guide

JANET & GEOFF BENGE

YWAM PUBLISHING
P.O. BOX 55787 SEATTLE, WA 98155

YWAM Publishing is the publishing ministry of Youth With A Mission. Youth With A Mission (YWAM) is an international missionary organization of Christians from many denominations dedicated to presenting Jesus Christ to this generation. To this end, YWAM has focused its efforts in three main areas: (1) training and equipping believers for their part in fulfilling the Great Commission (Matthew 28:19), (2) personal evangelism, and (3) mercy ministry (medical and relief work).

For a free catalog of books and materials, contact:

YWAM Publishing
P.O. Box 55787, Seattle, WA 98155
(425) 771-1153 or (800) 922-2143
www.ywampublishing.com

Cameron Townsend: A Unit Study Curriculum Guide

10 09 08 07 06 05 04 10 9 8 7 6 5 4 3 2 1

Published by Youth With A Mission Publishing
P.O. Box 55787
Seattle, WA 98155

ISBN 1-57658-278-7

Printed in Germany.

Contents

CAMERON TOWNSEND

1896–1982

Cameron Townsend: A Unit Study Curriculum Guide

This unit study guide is designed to accompany the book *Cameron Townsend: Good News in Every Language* from the Christian Heroes: Then & Now series by Janet and Geoff Benge. It provides the Christian schoolteacher and homeschooling parent with ways to use the book as a vehicle for teaching or reinforcing various curriculum areas, including

- Creative writing.
- Drama.
- Movie critiquing.
- Reading comprehension.
- Essay writing.
- History and geography concepts.

Since there are more ideas than could possibly be used in one unit, it is the parent/teacher's job to sift through the ideas and select those that best fit the needs of the student or students.

The activities recommended in this unit study guide are

- Reflective of a wide range of learning styles.
- Designed for both group and individual study.
- Suitable for a range of grade levels and abilities.

Learning Styles

Choose those activities that are best suited to your student or students. For example, when studying the physical features of a country, a kinesthetic learner will learn best by producing a three-dimensional clay model representing the physical features of the country, whereas a visual learner will find it more meaningful to produce a poster map of the country for the classroom wall.

Group or Individual Study

While the activities contained in this unit study guide are designed to be carried out by a student working alone, instructions are also provided for adapting an activity for a group.

Grade Levels/Abilities

As you thumb through this unit study guide, you will note that grade levels are not assigned to particular activities, though some areas—essay topics, for example—progress from the simple to the complex. This approach has been taken because students of varying grade levels can undertake most of the activities. For example, one of the activities suggests, "Using the websites listed in the Books and Resources section, design a poster or brochure to encourage people to join

Wycliffe. Make sure it answers some of the basic questions an inquirer might have." A third grader undertaking this project would probably produce a simple message, such as "Every person needs a Bible to read," and answer questions like "Where would I go?" and "How long would I be gone?" In contrast, a tenth grader would be able to include statistics on what portion of the world is still without a written language, the rate at which indigenous languages are being recorded, and projections of when the work of recording every language will be completed. Each student uses the same activities and instructions to create work appropriate to his or her age and cognitive ability.

In the center of this unit study guide you will find two foldout pages. These pages contain three maps and a fact sheet to be filled out by the student. The maps and fact sheet are designed to be photocopied onto individual pages so that each student can store them in his or her folder. They are for use with the social studies section of this unit study guide (chapter 6).

Before you begin teaching from this unit study guide, please read through each section. You may wish to highlight the activities that appeal to you or that your students would enjoy or be challenged by. Many teachers find it useful to plan the culminating event (see chapter 8) first and then select a range of learning activities that lend themselves to this event.

For the sake of brevity in the instructions that accompany each section, the word *teacher* includes the homeschooling parent, and the word *student* refers to a child either in a traditional classroom or in a homeschool environment.

1

Key Bible Verses

The authors have selected four Bible verses that can be used alongside or as part of this unit study. For your convenience, these verses have been quoted in two versions: the King James Version and the New International Version. Of course, many other appropriate Bible verses can be added to the list if more are needed. The verses could be used in the following ways:

Memorization. The teacher can assign one or all of the verses to be memorized during the course of the study. A chart could track which students have memorized which verses.

Meaning. The verses can be used to spark conversations on the spiritual aspects of Cameron Townsend's life. This can then be translated into action by having students form groups and present one of the verses to the class in a creative manner. Students could make up a skit to illustrate the meaning of the verse or present a one-act play to illustrate how the verse was relevant in the life of Cameron Townsend.

Devotional. The teacher might consider beginning a class or family devotional book. To do this, the teacher should familiarize the students with a variety of devotional writings and then ask them to write a devotion based upon their own understanding of one of the verses as it relates to the life of Cameron Townsend. The pages could then be glued or copied into a blank book, illustrated, and signed. The various devotions could be read aloud at appropriate times, including during assemblies, family devotional times, and the culminating event.

Display. Students could design a plaque, wall hanging, or banner, with one of the verses written on it. This could be hung in a prominent place while the unit study is under way and used for decoration during the culminating event.

“For the earth shall be filled with the knowledge of the glory of the LORD, as the waters cover the sea” (Habakkuk 2:14 KJV).

“For the earth will be filled with the knowledge of the glory of the LORD, as the waters cover the sea” (Habakkuk 2:14 NIV).

(This is the verse Cameron Townsend's father quoted at the end of the family's morning devotions.)

“But Jesus beheld them, and said unto them, With men this is impossible; but with God all things are possible” (Matthew 19:26 KJV).

“Jesus looked at them and said, ‘With man this is impossible, but with God all things are possible’” (Matthew 19:26 NIV).

“What man of you, having an hundred sheep, if he lose one of them, doth not leave the ninety and nine in the wilderness, and go after that which is lost, until he find it?” (Luke 15:4 KJV)

“Suppose one of you has a hundred sheep and loses one of them. Does he not leave the ninety-nine in the open country and go after the lost sheep until he finds it?” (Luke 15:4 NIV)

“For the word of God is quick, and powerful, and sharper than any twoedged sword, piercing even to the dividing asunder of soul and spirit, and of the joints and marrow, and is a discerner of the thoughts and intents of the heart” (Hebrews 4:12 KJV).

“For the word of God is living and active. Sharper than any double-edged sword, it penetrates even to dividing soul and spirit, joints and marrow; it judges the thoughts and attitudes of the heart” (Hebrews 4:12 NIV).

2

Display Corner

Many students will enjoy collecting and displaying objects related to the country or culture they are studying. It is motivational to designate a corner of the room, including a table or desk and wall space, that can be used for this purpose. Keep some index cards on the table and encourage students to label their contributions, including as much information as possible about where each object came from, what it is used for, and who would use it.

Encourage students to ask their parents and friends if they have anything interesting (but not valuable) from Mexico, Central America, or South America that they could bring to class. A visit to an Hispanic grocery could also yield some interesting display items, as would a trip to the local library to find books on Mexico and famous Mexican people and events. (See the Books and Resources section for ideas.)

Following is a list of items students (or you) might like to display. Of course, there are many more options.

- A large map of Mexico and of Central and South America
- Various Central and South American flags
- Picture books of Mexico and of Central and South America
- Examples of Bible tracts or Bibles written in other languages (available through the American Bible Society at (800) 32-BIBLE or online at www.americanbible.org)
- A tape recorder with a tape of various people reading Bible verses in several foreign languages (See if the students can guess what the languages are.)
- Food from Mexico and Central and South America (A plate of the Tetelcingo diet of beans, tortillas, and chilies would be interesting.)
- Dolls in native Mexican dress
- A map of the world featuring people groups who still do not have a written language
- A chart of all the languages that students in your class speak or hear on a regular basis (You will need to ask them what languages their relatives and neighbors speak.)
- Postcards, posters, calendars, and books about Wycliffe Bible Translators and JAARs, and copies of *In Other Words*, the official Wycliffe magazine (Order a catalog at (800) 992-5433 or visit the website at www.wycliffe.org/catalog. You can also see the Books and Resources section of this unit guide for details on acquiring these.)
- Newspaper articles that highlight current events related to Mexico or indigenous languages
- Mexican stamps and coins

3

Chapter Questions

There are four questions related to each chapter of *Cameron Townsend: Good News in Every Language:*

1. A vocabulary question drawn from the text and referenced to a page in the book
2. A factual question arising from the text
3. A question to gauge the level of a student's comprehension
4. An open-ended question seeking an opinion or interpretation

These questions are designed for students to complete on their own. They are best answered as a student finishes reading each chapter in the book. Answers to the first three questions for each chapter are given in Appendix B of this guide. The answer to the fourth question is open-ended and needs to be evaluated separately. Since question four deals with a student's interpretation or opinions, it is a good question on which to base a group discussion. Keep in mind that there are no right or wrong answers to question four, only positions a student should be able to justify.

To gain maximum benefit from the questions, the students should write full-sentence answers and not just one or two words. For example, in response to the question "Where did Cam meet President Nixon?" they should write, "Cam met President Nixon in the Oval Office of the White House," and not simply "the White House."

Each vocabulary question asks the students to use the new word in a sentence. Make sure that their sentences clearly demonstrate the meaning of the vocabulary word.

As a supplement to answering the questions, students may write a short summary of each chapter or write a response to the chapter in their journal. This could involve the students writing about how they relate to Cameron Townsend's actions, noting how they think they would react in a similar situation, and speculating as to what might happen next in the story.

Chapter One

1. What does *plush* mean (page 10)? Use this word in a sentence.
2. Where did Cam meet President Nixon?
3. How does the reader know that Wycliffe Bible Translators was a well-established organization at the time Cam met President Nixon?
4. Cam "wouldn't have changed the course of his life for anything" (page 11). What do you think was the source of his contentment? Explain your answer.

Chapter Two

1. What does *ramshackle* mean (page 15)? Use this word in a sentence.

2. What was Cam's original career goal?
3. In what way did Cam's near-drowning experience cause him to feel "older and wiser" (page 20)?
4. Compare the value placed on attending high school in 1910 with the views on high school today. What do you think accounts for these differences?

Chapter Three

1. What does *frugal* mean (page 23)? Use this word in a sentence.
2. What happened during Cam's third year of college that made his future seem uncertain?
3. Why did Cam think there was no way he could get out of going to France to fight?
4. Put yourself in the place of the captain of Cam's National Guard unit. Would you discharge Cam to sell Bibles in Central America or send him to fight Germany in World War I? Why?

Chapter Four

1. What does *treacherous* mean (page 39)? Use this word in a sentence.
2. What Spanish word does the name Cameron sound like?
3. Why was Cam dismayed when he realized that he had never shared his faith with a non-Christian?
4. Attending the Bible conference was an eye-opening experience for Cam. In your opinion, what does it mean to be a missionary?

Chapter Five

1. What does *inquisitive* mean (page 46)? Use this word in a sentence.

2. Who was the first person whose conversion Cam played a part in?
3. Why was the mayor of Chimaltenango relieved when Cam told him about the Bibles and how he wanted to help the people in the town?
4. What unique challenges would missionaries face in Guatemala, a country so steeped in superstition?

Chapter Six

1. What does *deliberation* mean (page 61)? Use this word in a sentence.
2. Who are the Ladinos?
3. What did Cam consider to be the cause of the tribe's superstitious lifestyle?
4. Cam was a very determined young man. Describe one scene in the chapter that depicts this trait.

Chapter Seven

1. What does *conscientious* mean (page 71)? Use this word in a sentence.
2. What did Mr. Treichler suggest that Cam could do to support a wife?
3. Why was the way Elvira responded to the Cakchiquel Indians so important to Cam's conclusion that she would make a wonderful wife?
4. What do you think would be the most challenging aspect of translating a language for the first time?

Chapter Eight

1. What does *unscathed* mean (page 81)? Use this word in a sentence.
2. Who was Mrs. Heim?
3. What change in the leaders' perspectives did Cam

hope would come as a result of the Protestant service at the Central American Congress?

4. What do you think would have been Cam's biggest struggle in going on with his work after Robby died? Explain your answer.

Chapter Nine

1. What does *commending* mean (page 95)? Use this word in a sentence.
2. What was the name of the Bible school that Cam opened in 1923?
3. Why was Cam's focus on Bible translation such a big concern to his mission board?
4. Why do you think Cam lost his temper with Mr. Smith?

Chapter Ten

1. What does *copious* mean (page 109)? Use this word in a sentence.
2. Whom did Cam meet on May 19, 1931?
3. Why was Cam disappointed by the letter from the leaders of the Central American Mission?
4. At the end of the chapter, everything seemed to be going wrong for Cam. Which of these challenges do you think would have shaken Cam's vision most? Explain your answer.

Chapter Eleven

1. What does *innovative* mean (page 122)? Use this word in a sentence.
2. What accomplishment was John Wycliffe known for?
3. What caused Rafael Ramírez to change his mind and grant Cam permission to stay in Mexico?

4. Do you think Cam should have stayed in Mexico even though he knew he could not do Bible translation work there at that time? Explain your answer.

Chapter Twelve

1. What is a prospectus (page 129)? Use this word in a sentence.
2. Why did Cam interrupt his tour of Mexican schools to go back to the United States?
3. Why did Cam ask the Church of the Open Door to stop supporting him financially?
4. Do you think you would have enrolled in Camp Wycliffe? Why or why not?

Chapter Thirteen

1. What does *agape* mean (page 142)? Use this word in a sentence.
2. Who traveled to Mexico with Cam and Elvira to act as a nurse for Elvira?
3. What is meant by the statement: "The noose had been tightening around the necks of missionaries" (page 139)?
4. What does Cam's reaction to Ken Pike's firewood hunt tell us about Cam?

Chapter Fourteen

1. What does *uncoupled* mean (page 151)? Use this word in a sentence.
2. What did Cam take with him to Mexico City to show officials what the Indians were capable of growing if they had a little help?
3. Why was President Cárdenas referred to as "the peasant's president"?

4. What do you think motivated Cam to serve the people of Tetelcingo beyond translating their language?

Chapter Fifteen

1. What does *stamina* mean (page 160)? Use this word in a sentence.
2. What two issues did L. L. and Cam disagree about at the third Camp Wycliffe?
3. What was unusual about the role of the director in the Summer Institute of Linguistics committee?
4. During the third Camp Wycliffe everyone followed Cam's nieces' example and called him "Uncle Cam." Why do you think this name stuck with him?

Chapter Sixteen

1. What does *fledgling* mean (page 178)? Use this word in a sentence.
2. Who was the first woman doctor in Guatemala?
3. What did Cam mean when he wrote, "The task she served, however, remains, and we remain" (page 176)?
4. What potential benefits might come as a result of a biography about President Cárdenas?

Chapter Seventeen

1. What does *aboriginal* mean (page 190)? Use this word in a sentence.
2. Where did Cam and Elaine's wedding take place?
3. Why did Dale Kietzman look stunned when Cam asked him to film the plane wreckage?
4. If you had been Cam or Elaine, would you have been willing to travel in a small plane again after a crash like theirs? Why or why not?

Chapter Eighteen

1. What is a pavilion (page 197)? Use this word in a sentence.
2. What was the title of the movie Cam edited about SIL?
3. Why was the pavilion at the World's Fair considered a success for SIL?
4. What do you think Cam meant by the statement, "The greatest missionary of all is the Bible in a person's own language"? Do you agree or disagree with this statement? Explain your answer.

Chapter Nineteen

1. What does *ideological* mean (page 206)? Use this word in a sentence.
2. What region of Russia did Cam and Elaine begin their translating work in?
3. Why was SIL one of the few foreign organizations invited to work in the Soviet Union?
4. Cam was in his seventies when he started to learn Russian. What do you think this shows about his character?

Chapter Twenty

1. What does *condolence* mean (page 219)? Use this word in a sentence.
2. On what date did Cam die?
3. The text says, "It was not surprising that after his death the work went on" (page 221). Why was it not surprising?
4. What would you consider to be Cam's most significant accomplishment in his lifetime?

4

Student Explorations

Student explorations are a variety of activities that are appropriate for a wide range of learning styles. These activities consist of the following:

Essay Questions. These are questions that can be used as ideas for writing essays. Students can either be assigned a topic or choose their own from the list. The simplest essay topics appear first, followed in order by those that are more complex.

Creative Writing. This includes various types of writing, such as newspaper articles, poems, letters, résumés, songs, and journals.

Hands-on Projects. These are various kinds of projects, such as charts and graphs, models, comic strips, family crests, mottoes, dioramas, book covers, and mobiles.

Audio/Visual Projects. These involve such activities as using a tape recorder to conduct a mock interview or to produce a radio play or commercial, or using still and video cameras to create dramatic presentations.

Arts and Crafts. These include art forms and crafts used in Mexico.

Language Examples. Some examples of words written in the Cakchiquel language are given. Students can use them to make banners or place mats for the culminating event or in their hands-on projects. For example, they could use them on an illustrated timeline of Cameron Townsend's life.

[Note on group projects: All the suggestions described below are individual learning activities. However, some of the activities have bracketed paragraphs like this one after them that offer suggestions on how the activity can be adapted for class or group use.]

Essay Questions

1. Cameron Townsend faced many obstacles as he sought to translate the Bible into unwritten languages. Name the three obstacles you think were the most challenging and explain how he overcame them.

2. Cameron Townsend was a lifelong learner. Explore how this trait contributed to the success of Wycliffe Bible Translators and SIL.

3. "Those who attain to any excellence commonly spend life in some single pursuit, for excellence is not gained upon easier terms." Use this quote from Samuel Johnson to comment on Cameron Townsend's life, vision, and accomplishments.

4. Although Cameron Townsend was raised in a poor environment, he was able to mix easily with wealthy people and individuals in high positions. What qualities do you think enabled him to do this? Explain, using examples from the book.

5. Cameron Townsend once said, "The greatest missionary of all is the Bible in a person's own language. It never needs a furlough, and it is never considered a foreigner." Interview three Christians you admire, and find out what role the Bible played in their conversion and continues to play in their faith. Write an essay explaining how their experiences relate to Cameron Townsend's statement.

6. Research an indigenous language of the area where you live, and write an essay explaining its history and either its current usage or when and why it died out.

Creative Writing

1. Imagine you were Elena Trejo when she was asked to give the speech in Mexico City (see page 171). Write what you think she might have said.

2. Choose a key event in Cameron Townsend's life, and write a newspaper article about it. For example, you might write about his decision to translate Scripture into the Cakchiquel language or the acquisition of a pavilion at the World's Fair. Be sure to include a catchy headline.

   [If you allocate different events to various students or groups of students, your class can create a single newspaper covering Cameron Townsend's life.]

3. Ken Pike told stories about what life was like in a remote Mexican village. Imagine that you are a knowledgeable and entertaining lecturer, and write a story about the people and places that surround you.

4. None of Cameron Townsend's family was able to attend his wedding to Elvira. Imagine you are Cam, and write a letter home to his parents describing their new daughter-in-law and the wedding.

5. Choose a period in Cameron Townsend's life that particularly interests you, and write a series of journal entries that Cam might have made during that time.
   [If you allocate different time periods to various students or groups of students, your class can create a single journal covering Cameron Townsend's life.]

Hands-on Projects

1. Make an illustrated timeline of Cameron Townsend's life that shows the major events involved in the establishment of Wycliffe Bible Translators and SIL, as well as major world events.
   [This can be an individual or a group effort.]

2. Design a logo for Wycliffe Bible Translators. Write a brief explanation of why you chose particular symbols, words, or letters.

3. Using the websites listed in the Books and Resources section, design a poster or brochure to encourage people to join Wycliffe. Make sure it answers some of the basic questions an inquirer might have.

4. Using papier-mâché or modeling clay, make a topographical model of Central America. Paint it and use toothpick flags to label the cities, rivers, mountains, neighboring countries, and seas. Put stars on the places where Cameron Townsend traveled and lived.

5. Draw and label a map of the world showing the regions where there are still people groups who do not have access to the Bible in their native language.
6. Using the information in the book and your own imagination, create a model of what you think the pavilion at the World's Fair might have looked like. Write a short explanation to go with it.
7. Create and perform a dance or mime celebrating the coming of God's Word to a people group.
8. Create either a comic strip or a children's story about a portion of Cameron Townsend's life that interests you.

Audio/Visual Projects

1. Research the life of the Bible translator John Wycliffe. From what you learn, write and film a documentary or drama about him and his work.
2. Create a television documentary called *Wycliffe: Its Past, Present, and Future*. Use the website www.wycliffe.org and others listed in the Books and Resources section for information.

   [This could be a group effort, with individual students or teams assigned to each of the three time periods.]
3. Imagine that a Wycliffe missionary is coming to your church or school. Create a video spot, a radio advertisement, or a computer slide show to pique people's interest in attending this event.
4. Research the Mexican creation myth. Stage a play or another dramatization based on this myth, and videotape the performance.

Arts and Crafts

1. Weaving is a traditional Latin American craft. This is normally done on a backstrap loom, but students could do a simple project using a subtle stick as a loom. (See the book *Fiesta! Guatemala*, page 24, for details and illustrations.)

2. Amerindian women often create brightly colored embroidery, which they use to decorate their clothing. Use a light-colored background and vivid colors of wool thread to make a traditional embroidery pattern.

3. Latin American Indians often use bright colors and bold shapes on felt wall hangings. Make a wall hanging with felt appliqué. (See the book *Fiesta! Guatemala*, page 18, for details and illustrations.)

4. Many Amerindian people prepare and eat their food out of pottery utensils and bowls. These are normally made by using either the slab or coil method, as pottery wheels are seldom used. Try using the slab or coil method to make a clay bowl.

5. Piñatas are often used as part of celebrations in Latin America. Using papier-mâché, create a piñata. This could be filled with candy and small prizes and used in the culminating event.

6. Learn and perform a traditional Mexican or Guatemalan folk dance.

Language Examples

Below are two Bible verses written in Cakchiquel, the first language Cameron Townsend recorded and translated the New Testament into.

Mark 16:15

"Y xubij chique: Quixbiyin chuvech ronojel ri ruvachulef; titzijoj ri utzilej rutzijol chique conojel ri vinek."

"He said to them, 'Go into all the world and preach the good news to all creation'" (NIV).

Romans 12:1

"QUE-CA-RI, vachalal nicutuj utzil chive roma ri e rujoyovabel ri Dois, chi quiehiya ri ichacul pa caslic camelabel, lokolej, dika chuvech ri Dois, chi jari ri isamaj riquin nahoj."

"Therefore, I urge you, brothers, in view of God's mercy, to offer your bodies as living sacrifices, holy and pleasing to God—this is your spiritual act of worship" (NIV).

5

Community Links

Many communities have a rich supply of people and places to which students can be exposed to help them learn about and appreciate other cultures. It is well worth the effort to find out what your community has to offer in regard to the unit you are studying.

If you are unable to take a field trip to visit some of these people and places, it is often possible to have visitors come to the classroom. Whether you take a field trip or invite someone to your classroom, such activities need to be flanked by sound educational choices; otherwise, much of the event's educational value will not be realized. The following three steps will help students derive the greatest educational value from a field trip or classroom visit.

Step One: Preparation

Students should always research the topic before they begin a field trip or classroom interview. In doing so, they will be ready to ask intelligent questions based upon a sound knowledge of their topic. For example, if the class is going to visit an Hispanic church, borrow a hymnbook ahead of time and show the students basic Spanish pronunciation. That way, they may be able to sing along and follow the Bible reading better.

As the teacher, you need to give the students a clear idea as to why they are going on the field trip and what they are expected to produce with their findings. For example, you might say to them, "We are going to visit an Hispanic church. When we get back, you will be writing an article for the school newsletter about your experience."

Prior to the event, students should be encouraged to compile lists of questions they want answers to, stemming from what they have already learned. They should carry a clipboard with them to write down answers, draw sketches, and note observations. (For less motivated students, a simple worksheet of activities to be completed on the field trip itself may be a good idea.) Such activities reinforce the idea that the field trip is a serious educational event and that the student is there to gather information, not just to be a sightseer. (If you are attending a church, the worksheet might be something you would want the students to fill out afterward, not during the service.)

Step Two: The Event

During the field trip or classroom visit, make sure that the students remain on task. Insist that they be respectful of property and other people at all times. Make sure that you have a spokesperson designated to thank whomever you talk to as well as the parents who help with the event.

Step Three: Processing and Reflection

Students should be given time to process the information they have gathered from their field trip or classroom visit and reflect on it, both individually and as a class. This can take many forms, including making flowcharts or diagrams of what they learned, editing interviews for articles or audiovisual presentations, writing reports, and making booklets. Something as simple as a class book called *Did You Know?*, in which each student writes down one fact he or she learned from the field trip, can serve as an effective reflection tool.

Suggested Community Links

Hispanic Church. Locate an Hispanic church in your area. Call the pastor and ask permission to take your class for a visit. (Attending a Sunday service would be ideal if you could arrange it with the students' families.) Be sure to find out if the church has a dress code or any special customs that the students (and you) should be aware of. If attending a Sunday service is not possible, ask if you can visit the pastor at the church on another day or if the pastor can come to school to speak to your class.

Mexican Restaurant. Arrange to visit a Mexican restaurant during a nonbusy time of the day. See if you can arrange ahead of time for the owner to talk to the class about preparing Mexican food. Eat lunch there, making sure the students try foods that are new to them.

Mexican or Central American People. People are some of the best resources of all. Are there any Mexican or Central American people in your town? (A local Hispanic church might be a good place to start.) Invite such a person to speak to the class. How long has his or her family been in the United States? What part of Mexico or Central America is his or her family originally from? Has he or she ever been back there to visit? If not, does he or she want to go back to visit?

People Who Have Visited Mexico or Central America. You may be able to locate someone who has visited Mexico or Central America. If so, invite him or her to show slides, photos, and other memorabilia from the trip.

A Missionary Who Has Worked in Mexico or Central America. If you can locate a missionary who has worked in Mexico or Central America, invite this person to your class to tell about his or her experiences.

Wycliffe Bible Translators. If you live near Orlando, Florida, Wycliffe Bible Translators USA has a magnificent facility for a field trip. It includes a movie theater, an interactive exhibit, an extensive bookstore, a tour, and the opportunity to meet and talk with a Wycliffe worker. Check Wycliffe's website at www.wycliffe.org for details.

Wycliffe or JAARS Worker/Representative. Both of these organizations have many speakers throughout the United States and other countries. You may be able to coordinate your unit study with a visit from one of these representatives. Check the website at www.wycliffe.org for details.

6

Social Studies

The social studies section is divided into five categories, each with suggestions for using the material given. The categories are briefly described below.

Places. This section covers significant places related to the story and named in the text of the book *Cameron Townsend: Good News in Every Language.*

Journey. This category covers one journey undertaken by Cameron Townsend.

Terms/Vocabulary. This section gives ideas for studying some of the terms used in the book.

Geographical Characteristics. This section contains suggestions for mapping some of the physical characteristics of Mexico.

Conceptual Questions. This section provides the teacher with conceptual social studies questions related to the book.

Places

These places are categorized by country, with the page number where they are first referred to in the book given in parentheses. Students can undertake a range of activities with these place names. They can

- Locate and mark the places on the relevant country map. (Maps for this purpose are located in the foldout section of this guide.)
- Note other points, such as their absolute location (latitude and longitude), then observe how this location compares to other locations mentioned in the book. For example, they can calculate which location is closer to the equator or to the North Pole.
- Calculate the relative locations of various places mentioned in the book. For example, how far is it from Los Angeles to Mexico City or from New York to Moscow?
- Explore how some of the place names have changed since the time of the story and give reasons for such changes.
- Pinpoint the places on a large wall map in the classroom. Students can then use index cards to write explanations as to why the various places are mentioned in the story. Each card could be pinned to the wall, with a length of yarn connecting it to the appropriate place on the map.

Places in the United States

Downey, California (11)
Fresno, California (13)
Los Angeles, California (14)
Long Beach, California (14)
Santa Ana, California (20)
Clearwater, California (21)
San Diego, California (23)
San Francisco, California (33)
New York City (40)
Chicago, Illinois (68)
Dallas, Texas (94)
Wichita Falls, Texas (116)
Laredo, Texas (118)
Sulphur Springs, Arkansas (128)
Glendale, California (133)
Hollywood, California (175)
Charlotte, North Carolina (197)

Places in Guatemala

San José (36)
Guatemala City (37)
Antigua (39)
San Antonia Aguas Calientes (43)
Santa Catarina Barahona (43)
Tecpan (43)
Santiago (44)
Chimaltenango (53)
Escuintla (56)
Comalapa (75)
Panajachel (82)
Guatalon (86)

Places in Mexico

Mexico City (117)
Monterrey (120)
Tamazunchale (143)
Tetelcingo (149)
Mazatec (167)
Tuxtla (183)

Other places

Vancouver, Canada (23)
Lima, Peru (185)
Moscow, Russia (207)
New Delhi, India (211)

Journey

Using Cameron Townsend's journey in 1969, students can

- Map the journey on the relevant map.
- Compare the journey Cam took to taking the same journey today. Students could research how they might reach those destinations today, how long it would take to get there, and how much it would cost.

Cameron's journey

Cam visited the following countries and states on his journey around the world:

North Carolina (210)
Soviet Union [Russia] (210)
India (211)
Nepal (211)
Philippines (211)
Papua New Guinea (211)

Australia (212)
New Zealand (212)
Hawaii (212)

Terms/Vocabulary

Following is a list of terms used in the book. The page number where the term is first used is in parentheses. The list covers terms ranging from the simple to the advanced. Students can use this list to

- Define and memorize the terms. You may find it helpful to asterisk or highlight in some way those terms you think are appropriate for your students. If they know the meaning of all but five of the terms, have them learn only those five. Conversely, if they are unfamiliar with most of the terms, choose a realistic number for each student to explore and learn.
- Produce an individual or class reference book of terms. Assign each student a number of terms to write a definition for or, where possible, depict in a sketch. From this research, a book of definitions can be made, allotting one page for each definition. This book could be added to throughout the year. (Students may need a dictionary to help them with this activity.)
- Play reinforcement games such as Go Fish. To do this, write some terms from the list below on index cards and have students take turns pairing them with sketches or definitions on other index cards.

Terms/vocabulary

irrigation (18)
canal (18)
culture (26)
tribes (29)

peninsula (35)
lighter boat (36)
ancestors (46)
mule train (46)
volcanoes (48)
peasants (50)
earthquake (59)
aftershocks (62)
influenza (63)
malaria (68)
archaeologist (74)
Amazon Basin (99)
Great Depression (100)
literacy (106)
rural (108)
tuberculosis (110)
linguistics (114)
revolution (115)
immigration (118)
ethnologist (121)
gringos (152)
jungle (176)
ravine (187)
embassy (207)
Iron Curtain (207)
bilingual (210)
time zones (212)
UNESCO (218)

Geographical Characteristics

Have students use an atlas to locate the following and mark them on the blank map of Mexico from the foldout section in the center of the book:

- The following eleven rivers in Mexico, their sources, and their courses: Balsas, Bravo del Norte (Rio Grande), Fuerte, Grande de Santiago, Grijalva, Hunaya, Lerma, Moctezuma, Pánuco, Papaloapan, and Yaqui
- The thirty-one Mexican states and the Federal District
- The eight major geographical regions: Mexican Plateau, Gulf Coastal Plain, Pacific Lowlands, Baja California Peninsula, Balsas Depression, Southern Highlands, Isthmus of Tehuantepec, and Chiapas Highlands
- The following lakes: Chapala, Cuitzeo, and Pátzcuaro

- The following cities: Mexico City, Guadalajara, Monterrey, Léon, Juárez, Tijuana, Zapopan, Mexicali, Culicacán, Acapulco, and the capitals of at least four other Mexican states
- The latitude and longitude lines that bisect Mexico
- The seas and oceans that border Mexico: Gulf of Mexico, Bay of Campeche, Gulf of California, and Pacific Ocean
- The countries Mexico shares borders with: the United States, Guatemala, and Belize
- Citlaltépetl, the highest point in Mexico at 18,700 feet (5,700 meters)

Conceptual Questions

The following questions are ordered from the simple to the complex. Using these questions, you could ask students to

- Write one or more paragraphs to answer each question.
- Present an oral report to the class on one of the questions.
- Discuss the answer(s) to a question or questions in a group context.

Questions to ponder

- Name and locate two countries that are larger than Mexico, two that are about the same size, and two that are smaller.
- How large is Mexico compared to the United States?

- What is the population of Mexico compared to the population of the United States? How fast is each growing? What are the racial profiles of both countries?
- Following the Mexican Revolution, there was much tension between the Mexican government and the Catholic Church. Using contemporary news articles and recent history books, explore the relations between the two today.
- Explore the past and present relationships between Mexico's indigenous tribes and the Mexican government.
- Locate the countries that border Mexico. Research whether these neighboring countries have friendly or strained relationships with Mexico, and why. In what ways have these countries been linked to each other in the past?

7

Related Themes to Explore

Any unit study has natural links to many other topics that can also be explored. While it is impossible to pursue all such links in this context, the spoke diagram on the next page shows some related topics that students might find interesting to study in conjunction with Cameron Townsend.

There are two ways you might like to integrate some of these links into your classroom. Some teachers and parents have the flexibility to choose the topics their students study and even alter their selections partway through the year. If you are able to do this, use the theme wheel to help identify other topics you might like to explore following this unit. For example, after studying Cameron Townsend, your class might become interested in World War I, the Great Depression, or unreached people groups around the world.

Other teachers and parents are locked in to a less flexible curriculum. If this is your situation, you may still have the ability to change the order in which various topics are taught. Look through the list of topics to see whether any coincide with topics you have already scheduled for later in the year. If so, consider teaching these topics closer to this unit so that cross-curriculum learning can take place.

CAMERON TOWNSEND

History

- The United States during World Wars I and II
- The Great Depression
- Compulsory education in the United States
- The Mexican Revolution

Current Events

- Life in Mexico today
- Native American language preservation
- Debate over bilingual education
- Literacy campaigns around the world

Math

- Graph of the people groups who have a Bible translation in their language compared to those who do not
- Statistics pertaining to the number of Bible translations completed and those being worked on, and the percentage of the world's languages they represent

Missions

- Bible translators such as John Wycliffe
- JAARS
- MAF (Missionary Aviation Fellowship)
- Individual Wycliffe missionaries

8

Culminating Event

As adults, we like to have a reason to learn something. We learn a new computer program so that we can balance our checking account, a song so that we can sing it at a wedding, or the rudiments of another language so that we are able to find our way around in a foreign country. Students have the same need for purpose in their learning. It is valid but not very motivating to tell a student that he or she needs to gather and learn information to pass a test or move up a grade. It is much more motivating for a student when he or she has some other, more meaningful goal in mind. This goal can be a specific forum through which each student can express his or her newly acquired knowledge. We believe that part of the teacher's role is to provide such a forum, which we call the culminating event.

As the name implies, the culminating event marks the end of the unit study and gives a sense of closure to the topic. It also serves to put the students' new knowledge into a larger context that can then be shared with others.

The culminating event can be as simple as inviting the class next door (or the homeschooled children down the street) to come hear poems and stories and view the students' written work. Conversely, the event could be as involved as hosting a parent/neighborhood fiesta featuring Mexican and Guatemalan songs, games, piñatas, plays, and presentations on the life and achievements of Cameron Townsend, the organizations he founded, and the places he served.

No matter how simple or elaborate the culminating event is, make sure you have the broad outline of it in mind before planning the other activities for your unit study, as they are integrally linked.

Idea Sparks

Food. Prepare and serve regional food. Most of what we consider to be Mexican food is actually Tex-Mex food, so try a few authentic Mexican or Guatemalan dishes. Mexicans serve tortillas with every meal. Other common foods are beans, squash, corn, avocados, onions, bananas, plantains, chilies, peppers, coconuts, pineapples, eggs, and rice. Meats include goat, beef, chicken, and pork. A meal could consist of tamales, flautas, and refried beans, with flan for dessert. You will find recipes and food supplies at www.mexconnect.com and http://guat.clark.st/recipes.htm.

Beverages. Coffee with a lot of sugar stirred into it and hot cocoa are popular drinks throughout Mexico. So are fruit juices or smoothies, which the Mexicans call "licudos." These are made by blending orange juice and fresh fruit.

Table Manners. Meals in Mexico are a time for talking and laughing. The people sit at tables. The oldest people present are normally served first. In the villages the people eat with either a spoon or a fork and use their hands as well. Coffee or hot chocolate is served at the end of the meal. When the meal is over, the conversation often continues for another hour or longer.

Music. Play traditional Mexican or Guatemalan music in the background to set the mood. This music can be either mariachi-style music, which has its roots in the Spanish colonial era, or the pre-Spanish pipe and drum music that is still popular in the Mexican countryside. (Many libraries stock ethnic music selections.)

Oral Presentations. Students can present poems, essays, reports, speeches, reviews, journals, and devotions that they have written during the course of the unit study.

Displays. Display other work, including artwork, map work, models, newspapers, and video interviews.

Clothing. Students could dress in traditional Mexican or Guatemalan clothing for this event. Women and girls wear plain colored, brightly woven, or embroidered clothing. Blouses are often white and flouncy; skirts are long and full. Women also wear bright shawls and brightly colored necklaces and bracelets. Traditionally women go barefoot. Men wear plain cotton shirts and pants. These are normally white or light in color. Their hats are wide-brimmed felt or straw sombreros. Men wear leather sandals. Both men and women wear ponchos for warmth and protection from the rain.

Cultural Activities. Play traditional Mexican or Guatemalan games. No fiesta is complete without a piñata.

Appendix A

Books and Resources

This appendix is divided into seven sections: (1) other biographies of Cameron Townsend, (2) related books, (3) related books in the Christian Heroes: Then & Now series, (4) related documentaries, (5) related articles from *National Geographic,* (6) related Internet sites, and (7) a related interactive CD.

Some of the books listed here are more difficult to obtain than others. If they are not available at your local Christian bookstore, many of the titles can be located in secondhand bookstores or on the Internet. Most of the titles are also available through the national interlibrary loan service. You can also check the website www.wycliffe.org or call (800) 992-5433 to request a Wycliffe catalog. The catalog and the website contain most of the resources listed below and many others, including posters, postcards, calendars, and the Wycliffe Bible Translators magazine *In Other Words.*

Some of the books about Cameron Townsend are written at a higher reading level than the books in the Christian Heroes: Then & Now series and would be interesting for a teacher to read for his or her own information and as background for the unit. Children learn best by example, so consider choosing one adult biography to read to enrich your own understanding of the topic. Resources for younger children are also included, making it easy for younger family members or less capable readers to participate in the unit study at their own level.

Other Biographies of Cameron Townsend

All the biographies listed on the bibliography page of *Cameron Townsend: Good News in Every Language* are listed here, as well as others that may be of interest. Each listing has basic information on how to locate the book, including its ISBN. The approximate intended age level of the reader is also given, along with the number of pages in each book and some comments to help you decide whether or not to include the book in your unit study.

TITLE:	*Uncle Cam*
Authors:	James and Marti Hefley
Publisher:	Wycliffe Bible Translators, 1984
ISBN:	0938978039
Age Level:	Adult, 285 pages

Synopsis: This is a thorough biography of Townsend and the work of Wycliffe Bible Translators. It has about fifty photographs, including some from Townsend's childhood and the first classes of SIL.

Comments: This biography is an easy read, and it presents a lot of detail in a lively manner. This would be a good choice if you want to learn more about Townsend's life.

TITLE: *A Thousand Trails*
Author: Hugh Steven
Publisher: CREDO Publishing Corp., 1984
ISBN: 0920479006
Age Level: Adult, easy reading, 224 pages

Synopsis: This is the personal journal of Townsend from 1917 to 1919. It describes the two years he spent in Guatemala selling Bibles (the time when he first felt called to translate the gospel into every language on earth). The author was a personal friend of Townsend, and he weaves a commentary of Townsend's life through the journal entries. The book contains eight photographs, most of which appear in *Uncle Cam*.

Comments: This journal reflects Townsend's gift for writing and his eye for the details of the various cultures and people he interacted with. This would be a challenging read for teenagers, who would be drawn into the life of this twenty-year-old adventurer for God.

TITLE: *Wycliffe in the Making: The Memoirs of W. Cameron Townsend, 1920–1933*
Author: Hugh Steven
Publisher: Harold Shaw, 2000
ISBN: 0877888906
Age Level: Adult, easy reading, 288 pages

Synopsis: As the title suggests, this book deals with Townsend's life from 1920 to 1933. The book is a mixture of Townsend's writing and commentary from the author.

Comments: This is a great book, especially if you want more detail on a particular event or time period. Townsend wrote in a natural style, so students should not find it difficult to understand. This book covers the time period after that of *A Thousand Trails*.

TITLE: *Doorway to the World: Mexico*
Author: Hugh Steven
Publisher: Harold Shaw, 2000
ISBN: 0877888914
Age Level: Adult, easy reading, 300 pages

Synopsis: This book uses over sixteen thousand letters and documents to tell the story of Townsend and Wycliffe Bible Translators from 1934 to 1947.

Comments: This book covers the time period after that of *Wycliffe in the Making: The Memoirs of W. Cameron Townsend, 1920–1933*. It will help to answer detailed questions that students might have.

TITLE: *Remember All the Way*
Authors: William Cameron Townsend and Richard S. Pittman
Publisher: Wycliffe Bible Translators, 1975
ISBN: None given
Age Level: Adult, easy reading, 144 pages

Synopsis: This book is a compilation of four- to six-page teachings, mainly by Townsend about missionary work.

Comments: This book would make an excellent devotional to read and discuss. The stories are well illustrated and make memorable points.

Related Books

Listed in this section are other books that fit around the life of Cameron Townsend. The listings include the ISBN, age level, and relevant comments.

Of course, there are many other books that relate in some way to this topic. Inside the back cover of this unit study guide, you may want to record the titles of other books you find particularly helpful.

TITLE: *Two Thousand Tongues to Go*
Authors: Ethel Wallis and Mary Bennett
Publisher: Harper & Brothers, 1959
ISBN: None given
Age Level: Adult, easy reading, 308 pages

Synopsis: This book uses numerous human interest stories to describe the development of Wycliffe Bible Translators. The first half of the book is contemporaneous with Townsend. It contains thirty-two pages of photographs, including some of Townsend, his growing family, and the first camps in Mexico.

Comments: *Two Thousand Tongues to Go* is quite a feat. This engaging story spans the world over a fifty-year period. It makes interesting reading in its entirety, although many of the chapters are cohesive enough to be read as stand-alones. Unfortunately, it does not have an index.

TITLE: *Independence and Revolution in Mexico, 1810–1940*
Author: Rebecca Stefoff
Publisher: Facts on File, Inc., 1993
ISBN: 0816028419
Age Level: 12 years and up, 150 pages

Synopsis: This is a brief, informative history of Mexico, including the time period when Townsend lived in the rural southern region.

Comments: This book is written in an engaging and straightforward manner. It deals with many complicated issues involving Mexico, Spain, France, and the United States. The land reforms of Townsend's friend President Cárdenas are covered thoroughly.

TITLE: *Cultures of the World: Mexico*
Author: Mary-Jo Reilly

Publisher: Benchmark Books, 1994
ISBN: 1854353853
Age Level: 9 years and up, 128 pages

Synopsis: Using photographs and text, this book deals with the following topics: geography, history, government, economy, environment, people, religion, language, arts, leisure, and food.

Comments: This is an appealing book about life in Mexico today. It gives a lot of information in an interesting manner.

TITLE: *Cultures of the World: Guatemala*
Author: Sean Sheehan
Publisher: Benchmark Books, 1998
ISBN: 0761408126
Age Level: 9 years and up, 128 pages

Synopsis: This book is part of the same series as *Cultures of the World: Mexico.* Using photographs and text, this book deals with the following topics: geography, history, government, economy, environment, people, religion, language, arts, leisure, and food.

Comments: This is an appealing book about life in Guatemala today. It gives a lot of information in an interesting manner.

TITLE: *Fiesta! Guatemala: A Portrait of the Country through Its Festivals and Traditions*
Editor: Tessa Paul
Publisher: Grolier Educational, 1999
ISBN: 0717293327
Age Level: 7 years and up, 32 pages

Synopsis: This book deals with various Guatemalan festivals and ways in which Guatemalan people celebrate their culture and heritage.

Comments: This is an outstanding resource book. As well as explaining how Guatemalans celebrate Christmas, Corn Festival, and All Saints' Day, it provides instructions for making simple food, woven bracelets, and wall hangings.

TITLE: *From Akebu to Zapotec: A Book of Bibleless Peoples*
Author: June Hathersmith; Illustrator: Alice Roder
Publisher: Wycliffe Bible Translators, 2002
ISBN: 0938978284
Age Level: 4 years and up, 32 pages

Synopsis: This book takes the reader on an alphabetical tour of people groups without the Bible in their native tongue. Each people group has a colorful illustration and a two-paragraph description.

Comments: Children will be drawn to the simple text and amazing illustrations in this book. It is great for younger children who are trying to grasp the idea of illiterate and/or unreached peoples of the world. This book is an update of *From Arapesh to Zuni*, as the languages depicted in that book have all now been translated.

TITLE: *What Language Does God Speak?*
Authors: Karen Lewis and Philip White
Publisher: Wycliffe Bible Translators, 1990
ISBN: None given
Age Level: 3 years and up, 16 pages

Synopsis: This coloring book gives children the opportunity to explore a real-life missionary/translator story. It deals with Jo Shelter and her work among the Balangao people in the Philippines.

Comments: This is a great way for younger children to understand the concept of Bible translation. The paper is high quality, and the illustrations and text are well done.

Related Christian Heroes: Then & Now Books

TITLE: *William Carey: Obliged to Go*
Authors: Janet and Geoff Benge
Publisher: YWAM Publishing, 1998
ISBN: 1576581470
Age Level: 10 years and up, 211 pages

Comments: William Carey (1761–1834) was one of the first missionaries to India. Although he had been a shoemaker with little formal schooling, he took on the task of translating the Bible into Bengali. Carey found that he had a gift for translation work, and he was eventually recognized as a leading Bengali and Sanskrit scholar.

TITLE: *Adoniram Judson: Bound for Burma*
Authors: Janet and Geoff Benge
Publisher: YWAM Publishing, 2000
ISBN: 1576581616
Age Level: 10 years and up, 232 pages

Comments: Adoniram Judson (1788–1850) was America's first foreign missionary. He overcame great personal trials and obstacles to translate the Bible into the Burmese language. The story of how his translation survived and was printed makes for exciting reading.

TITLE: *Betty Greene: Wings to Serve*
Authors: Janet and Geoff Benge
Publisher: YWAM Publishing, 1999
ISBN: 1576581527
Age Level: 10 years and up, 193 pages

Comments: Betty Greene was a World War II pilot who co-founded Missionary Aviation Fellowship. In 1945, Townsend recruited her to work with Wycliffe for a short period. Betty's story helps to fill in some of the details about the early flying days of Wycliffe Bible Translators.

Related Documentaries

Listed in this section are documentaries relevant to the life of Cameron Townsend. As with all unfamiliar material, it is prudent to preview movies before showing them to the class.

Documentaries are particularly useful in showing the visual details of another place and time period. As students watch, encourage them to study the clothing, weather, crops, terrain, and other geographical factors shown in the documentary.

TITLE: *A Flower Unfolds* and *The Ultimate Goal*
Publisher: Wycliffe Bible Translators
Type: Documentary
Length: 17 minutes
Year: 2002

Comments: This short two-part video celebrates Wycliffe Bible Translators' translation of the New Testament into its five hundredth language: Suriname Javanese. The first half of the documentary shows the excitement of these people to receive God's word in their own language. The second half of the video deals with Wycliffe's goal of translating the Bible in order to introduce people to God.

TITLE: *The Word Like a River*
Publisher: Wycliffe Bible Translators
Type: Documentary
Length: 20 minutes
Year: 1998

Comments: This is an overview of Wycliffe's work around the world. The documentary shows how translators work with the local people and how those local people react to having the New Testament in their own language. It is available in English and Spanish.

TITLE: *The Salsa-riffic World of Spanish Part 1*
Publisher: Standard Deviants
Type: Humorous/Instructional
Length: 90 minutes
Year: 2000

Comments: This is a fun introduction to the Spanish language. The video covers basic pronunciation, the Spanish alphabet, counting to ninety-nine, gender and nouns, and simple conversations. It will help students understand that translating something from one language to another is not merely a matter of exchanging one word for another.

TITLE: *Mexico: Journey to the Sun*
Publisher: Video Travel Library
Type: Documentary
Length: 53 minutes
Year: 1994

Comments: This video covers a wide range of facts about Mexico, but it is especially strong in the area of pre-Spanish history. It is a little dry in places, but it is well worth showing portions of it to a younger audience or showing it in its entirety to older students.

Related *National Geographic* Articles

Many magazines have articles related to this topic. We have chosen to reference *National Geographic* because it can provide contemporaneous commentary on many events and because it is widely available in libraries and schools throughout the country. (*National Geographic* magazines from 1888–2000 are available in their entirety on a CD-ROM set.)

These articles and their accompanying photographs represent just some of those available that bear on aspects of Cameron Townsend's life. They can be used in a variety of ways to support and reinforce this unit study. For example, you could have students read the May 1914 article "A Mexican Hacienda" and have them compare and contrast the author's observations of the system with Cameron Townsend's observations from the book. Or you could have a student read the December 1934 article "Travels with a Donkey in Mexico" and turn it into a dramatic monologue to be performed for the class.

Articles related to Mexico

TITLE: "Some Mexican Transportation Scenes"
Issue Date: December 1910, pages 985–991

Description: This is an interesting article with lots of photographs. It is about common forms of transportation in Mexico at the time, especially mule trains, which Townsend often used.

TITLE: "A Mexican Hacienda"
Issue Date: May 1914, pages 563–584

Description: This article describes the hacienda system (similar to the baron/serf system of medieval England). It explores the social, economic, and educational implications of haciendas, which Townsend was very concerned about. It contains great black-and-white pictures of rural people.

TITLE: "Our Neighbor, Mexico"
Issue Date: May 1911, pages 475–508

Description: This is a good general article about Mexico that includes information on topography, history, government, culture, and education.

TITLE: “Along the Old Spanish Road in Mexico”
Issue Date: March 1923, pages 225–281

Description: The Old Spanish Road is the oldest road on the North American continent. This is a rambling story about two men exploring this road that winds through rural Mexico. It contains interesting photographs and observations of people.

TITLE: “Travels with a Donkey in Mexico”
Issue Date: December 1934, pages 757–788

Description: This article is an often-humorous description of three Americans traveling through rural Mexico with two donkeys and a donkey driver. This article is contemporaneous with the time Townsend started his work in Mexico.

TITLE: “Modern Progress and Age-Old Glamour in Mexico”
Issue Date: December 1934, pages 741–756

Description: This article is made up of full-page photographs and captions on “modern progress” in and around Mexico City. It is contemporaneous with Townsend’s time there.

TITLE: “Popocatépetl: Mexico’s Smoking Mountain”
Issue Date: January 1999, pages 118–137

Description: This is a general article about life in southern Mexico under the shadow of the volcano Popocatépetl. The article also deals with syncretistic religious ceremonies that some believe will placate the volcano.

Articles related to Guatemala

TITLE: “Guatemala Interlude”
Issue Date: October 1936, pages 428–460

Description: This article provides a look at everyday life in the city and the country in Guatemala. The article shows crafts and a great photograph of people being "unloaded" from a ship in the same manner that is described in the book.

TITLE: "To Market in Guatemala"
Issue Date: July 1945, pages 87–104

Description: This article gives a brief history of Guatemala, including "modern" scenes. It is a good general overview of the country, and it contains hand-tinted color photographs.

Other related subjects

TITLE: "The Fractured Caucasus"
Issue Date: February 1996, pages 126–131

Description: The translation of languages in the Caucasus region was a challenge Townsend took on in old age. This article gives a good description of how fifty distinct languages came to exist in such a small area of the world. It includes a map showing the various languages.

TITLE: "The World's Words"
Issue Date: December 1943, pages 689–700

Description: This is an excellent article about the etymology of words, how languages are spread, and how English was becoming the dominant language. It includes basic information on translation techniques that were used at the same time Wycliffe was developing its own techniques.

Related Internet Sites

The following websites may have been updated since this guide was published, and as a result, they may contain information not reviewed here. Because of this, it is vital that you investigate them before allowing your students to view them.

www.wycliffe.org

This is Wycliffe Bible Translators' official website. It is very professional and carries a wide range of feature stories, testimonies, introductions to various translators, and prayer points. Visitors can also try the simulated translation work, take a linguistic aptitude test, and learn how to get involved with Wycliffe on some level. The site also has the online catalog of all Wycliffe products, including a wide assortment of books, videos, posters, postcards, calendars, crafts, and CDs for all age groups. Wycliffe can also be contacted at the following address: Wycliffe Bible Translators, P.O. Box 628200, Orlando, FL 32862-8200. Phone: (407) 852-3600 or (800) 992-5433.

www.jaars.org

JAARS is the sister organization of Wycliffe. The website deals with missionary aviation and is divided into sections on technology, ministry opportunities, the vernacular media, and logistics. There is a wide array of resources at this site, including opportunities for short-term missions, church and Sunday school programs, books, videos, and current projects. The organization can also be reached at the following address: JAARS, P.O. Box 248, Waxhaw, NC 28173. Phone: (704) 843-6000 or (800) 890-0628.

www.bazarmexico.com

This website sells a wide array of Mexican arts and crafts.

www.mexconnect.com

This website has many Mexican recipes and a store to buy traditional ingredients online.

http://guat.clark.st/recipes.htm

This website has a wide range of easy-to-understand Guatemalan recipes.

www.chick.com

This website has Bible tracts in a wide range of languages that can be downloaded or purchased.

www.worldscriptures.org

This is a great website. It uses graphs and maps to show the progress in Bible translation around the world today. It also has an extensive list of languages that have been translated and examples of what the first verses of the Gospel of John look like in those languages. If you click on Cakchiquel, you will find the "Townsend" version.

Related Interactive CD

Wycliffe Bible Translators also produces an interactive CD called *Great Commission Tool Box*. This CD includes all the ideas in the previously published *Bright Ideas* mission education ring binders. The CD is well worth purchasing, as it has missions-related simulation games, stories, and discussion materials for preschoolers through adults.

Appendix B

Answers to Chapter Questions

Chapter One

1. *Plush* means lavish or luxurious.
2. Cam met President Nixon in the Oval Office of the White House.
3. The reader knows it was a well-established organization because it had begun translating the Bible into its five hundredth language.

Chapter Two

1. *Ramshackle* means in a state of disrepair.
2. Cam's original career goal was to become a schoolteacher.
3. Cam's near-drowning experience caused him to think about life and death and reevaluate his priorities.

Chapter Three

1. *Frugal* means thrifty or economical.
2. During Cam's third year of college, the United States entered World War I.
3. Cam thought he couldn't avoid going to France because the National Guard rarely discharged able-bodied men.

Chapter Four

1. *Treacherous* means dangerous.
2. The name Cameron sounds like the Spanish word for shrimp.
3. He was dismayed that he had overlooked such an important part of the Christian faith, especially since as a missionary he would be expected to share his faith.

Chapter Five

1. *Inquisitive* means curious.
2. Tiburcio was the first person whose conversion Cam played a part in.
3. The mayor was relieved because he had been worried that Cam was going to complain about the "welcome" he received.

Chapter Six

1. *Deliberation* means careful consideration about all sides of an issue.
2. Ladinos are Guatemalan people who are part Spanish and part Indian.
3. Cam attributed the tribe's superstitious lifestyle to the lack of a written language of their own and a lack of scientific knowledge.

Chapter Seven

1. *Conscientious* means guided by conscience.
2. Mr. Treichler suggested that Cam join the Central American Mission as a way to support a wife.
3. The way Elvira responded to the Cakchiquel Indians was so important to Cam because he wanted to marry someone who would work effectively alongside him on the mission field.

Chapter Eight

1. *Unscathed* means unharmed.
2. Mrs. Heim was Cam's fifth-grade Sunday school teacher.
3. Cam hoped that the Central American leaders would realize that Indians could learn to read and write in their own language.

Chapter Nine

1. *Commending* means praising or speaking well of.
2. The Bible school was named the Robinson Bible Institute.
3. Cam's focus on Bible translation was such a big concern because previously translation had not been considered part of a missionary's role.

Chapter Ten

1. *Copious* means many or plentiful.
2. Cam met Guatemalan President Ubico on May 19, 1931.
3. Cam was disappointed by the letter because he had hoped for permission to begin working with another tribe who didn't yet have the Scriptures in their own language.

Chapter Eleven

1. *Innovative* means new and groundbreaking.
2. John Wycliffe was known for translating the Bible from Latin into English.
3. Rafael Ramírez changed his mind because he discovered that Dr. Tannenbaum endorsed Cam's work.

Chapter Twelve

1. A prospectus is a printed plan that is distributed to potential participants.
2. Cam interrupted his tour because he learned that Elvira was not expected to live for more than a few days.
3. Cam realized that with the religious opposition in Mexico, it would be to his advantage to enter the country as a linguist without direct ties to a church.

Chapter Thirteen

1. *Agape* means wide open.
2. Cam's niece, Evelyn Griset, traveled to Mexico with them.
3. This statement means that the government's restrictions were causing increasing difficulties for missionaries in Mexico.

Chapter Fourteen

1. *Uncoupled* means detached or disconnected.
2. Cam took heads of lettuce with him to show the officials in Mexico City what the Indians were capable of growing.
3. President Cárdenas was referred to as "the peasant's president" because he was concerned about the welfare of the poor in Mexico.

Chapter Fifteen

1. *Stamina* means endurance.
2. Cam and L.L. disagreed about the admittance of single women into the camp and having Ken Pike as one of the lecturers.
3. The director did not have the final say in any decision made by the Summer Institute of Linguistics committee.

Chapter Sixteen

1. *Fledgling* means young or inexperienced.
2. Elena Trejo was the first woman doctor in Guatemala.
3. Cam meant that there was still translation work to be done in Latin America and it was up to those who were still alive to continue the job.

Chapter Seventeen

1. *Aboriginal* means relating to the native people of Australia.
2. Cam and Elaine's wedding took place at the home of Lázaro and Amalia Cárdenas, west of Mexico City.
3. Dale was stunned because even though Cam was seriously injured, he was still thinking of ways this experience could benefit the mission.

Chapter Eighteen

1. A pavilion is an exhibition area.
2. The title of the movie was *Oh for a Thousand Tongues*.
3. The pavilion was considered a success because of the new recruits and the media attention it attracted.

Chapter Nineteen

1. *Ideological* means having to do with the beliefs or ideas of a group or culture.
2. Cam and Elaine began their work in the Caucasus region.
3. SIL was invited to work in the Soviet Union because of the positive relationships Cam had formed in other countries.

Chapter Twenty

1. *Condolence* means sympathy with another's grief.
2. Cam died on April 23, 1982.
3. It was not surprising that the work went on because Cam had spent his entire adult life sharing his vision and equipping people to carry it out.